I HATE **DUKE**®
303 Reasons Why You Should, Too

I HATE DUKE
303 Reasons Why You Should, Too

Paul Finebaum

CRANE HILL
P U B L I S H E R S

Birmingham, Alabama

Library of Congress Cataloging-in-Publication Data

Finebaum, Paul, 1955-
   I hate Duke: 303 reasons why you should, too / by Paul Finebaum
      p.   cm.
   ISBN 1-57587-147-5
   1.   Duke University — Football — Miscellanea.   I. Title.
GV958.D85F55   1995
796.332'63'097565--dc20   95-44378
                                                                  CIP

10   9   8   7   6   5   4   3   2

I HATE DUKE

I Hate Duke Because…

1. Richard Nixon graduated from Duke Law School—need we say more?

2. The captain of the Blue Devils cheerleading squad has a 40-inch bust and an I.Q. to match.

3. Like Tommy Lee, Cherokee Parks learned everything he knows in the back seat of a car.

4. Heather Sue Mercer's favorite food is thirds.

5. Carl Franks is a poster child for "a brain is an intelligent thing to waste" campaign.

6. The best Duke wannabes can get on their SATs is drool.

7. If Christian Laettner ever loses his current job, he can always get one in the police department for line-ups.

8. To get votes from the right wing voters in North Carolina, Jesse Helms promised to eat the lunches of underprivileged school children.

9. While dining in a Durham McDonald's, Coach K was overheard telling one of his bodyguards, "If they put condoms in here, this really would be a Happy Meal."

10. The top five most admired men by Duke students: Austin Powers.

11. Marilyn Manson.

12. Slim Shady.

13. Bill Clinton.

14. Paul Finebaum.

15. Duke administrators planted ivy on the campus in hopes they would be invited to join the Ivy League.

16. What do former coaches Red Wilson and Barry Wilson have in common? They both coached two years too many.

17. A good-looking Duke coed is obviously a visitor.

18. Even Divine Brown wouldn't work the corner of Wannamaker and Chapel Drive.

19. Most fans think Coach K should be given a high dose of Ritalin and sent home.

20. The good thing about Duke home games is there are always plenty of seats available.

21. The best form of birth control for Duke students: nudity.

22. A diploma from Duke is about as valuable as Duke football tickets.

23. *Playboy* featured a Blue Devil in its series "Girls in the ACC," because the Duke coeds were too ugly.

24. Five misconceptions students have about the value of their Duke diploma: They will find a job.

25. They will find a job in Washington.

26. They will find a job that won't require a hair net.

27. They will be respected by their peers.

28. They will immediately receive a free membership in the Sausage of the Month club.

29. Five things students can actually do with their Duke diploma: Get invited to Ted Kennedy's summer beach bash.

30. Work in the White House as Bill Clinton's hair stylist.

31. Work in the White House as Bill Clinton's runner for McDonald's.

32. Join the CIA–as a mail sorter.

33. Return to Duke as the head football coach–they'll hire anyone.

34. What do Carl Franks and Bill Clinton have in common? Both should be looking for new jobs.

35. Coach K will be teaching a mass communications course at Duke titled "The most ignorant things to say on national television."

36. *The Chronicle* would be a much better paper without Duke students.

37. Watching Duke football is about as exciting as the first half of the 1998-99 NBA season.

38. Bill Clinton is teaching a course at Duke titled "How to handle a woman."

39. More than 85 percent of Duke graduates and their families have been guests on "The Jerry Springer Show."

40. Duke football has always been known for upholding tradition—a losing tradition.

41. Instead of a whistle, the Duke-NC State game now will have to be started with a burglar alarm.

42. Instead of burning bras on campus, Duke football fans burn the NCAA rule book.

43. Coach K had an inferiority complex when it came to Dean Smith. He was cured after his shrink told him he really was inferior.

44. Most county jails in Durham installed Coach K's home number on their speed dial to better deal with Duke basketball players after being arrested.

45. The Duke Alumni Association offered Coach K an all-expense paid visit to Dr. Kevorkian.

46. The most popular drug for the Blue Devil coaching staff is Geritol.

47. Coach K is a weenie.

48. A major bone of contention among Duke fans getting a divorce is who gets to keep the trailer.

49. The second is who gets to keep the Dean Smith dart board.

50. The third is who gets to keep the video of Coach K's back surgery.

51. What is blue and white, 100 yards long, and has two front teeth? The front row at Wallace Wade Stadium.

52. Carl Franks winning national coach of the year is as impressive as Monica Lewinsky's cigar collection.

53. The only thing more obnoxious than a Duke fan is two Duke fans.

54. The I.Q. of the Blue Devil football team is somewhere between a house plant and an eggplant.

55. Some Duke athletes have taken more drug tests than academic exams.

56. The Duke undergraduate school has a class in "The best way to use your one phone call in jail."

57. In Poland they tell Duke jokes.

58. Duke is considering playing all future football games at night. That way it wouldn't be just the administration that is in the dark.

59. Why is it so hot during Blue Devil football games? Because there's not a fan in the place.

60. The Blue Devil has more teeth than the entire student body.

61. After visiting the Duke campus, Bill Clinton said, "This is the only school where the mascot looks better than the coeds."

62. *Gone With the Wind* is a famous movie about the South. But it's also what happens to most Duke fans' trailers during a tornado.

63. The mating call for Duke sorority members: "Ya'll, I'm drunk!"

64. Duke players smoke so much grass that once a month they have to get their stomachs mowed.

65. The campus bookstore even has marijuana-flavored mouthwash.

66. Coach K once said, "Marriage is a good way for guys to keep busy until the right girl comes along."

67. When Duke players are asked in a bar if they want Bud Light or Bud Dry, they normally respond, "Both."

68. Duke coaches quit trying to recruit players from high school. Instead, they just wait outside juvenile detention centers and sign the players there.

69. Duke is considering changing their cable broadcasts from CBS to the Prison Network so more of their former players can tune in.

70. The most exercise Carl Franks gets on a daily basis is pushing himself away from the table.

71. Duke has put almost as many players in the NBA draft in the last 10 years as any school in the ACC.

72. And more players in jail.

73. By the end of the decade, Duke may have as many candidates for the electric chair as Heisman contenders.

74. Instead of the team of the decade, Duke officials are considering putting together the best players at every position who are now serving time in the state penitentiary.

75. When Duke players get married, instead of registering china, some have been known to register for certain brands of bongs.

76. It's a good thing Duke football fans don't have to pass an I.Q. test to become season ticket holders.

77. Immediately after the UNC game, Coach K was found peeping inside the school newspaper's window.

78. Carl Franks once a gave a friend a cold just by sitting next to him.

79. The movie *Titanic* was loosely based on Frank's coaching in the FSU game.

80. Coach K has been known to nap during halftime of big games.

81. Duke has an announcer whose four favorite words are "All You Can Eat."

82. Coach K has a blow-up dummy of Dean Smith in his office.

83. The FAA has quit using dental records to identify Duke fans after plane crashes, because they don't have enough teeth.

84. Coach K once asked the Blue Devil for a date.

85. An academic All-American at Duke is someone who goes to class once a semester.

86. Duke fans have written their congressmen to request that the next nuclear test site be the NCAA headquarters.

87. Paul Finebaum is to Duke football what Rush Limbaugh is to Bill Clinton.

88. Word in Durham is don't ever invite Coach K and Bob Knight to the same picnic unless plastic knives are being used.

89. Fans are no longer allowed to have cellular phones in Wallace Wade Stadium because of the number of calls made to 911 after plays were made.

90. Coach Bob Trott's new book *All I Know About Coaching the Offensive Line* is blank.

91. If Carl Franks died during a football game, how would anyone know?

92. Johnny Dawkins's brain was rejected by an organ bank.

93. The reason Coach K never drinks anymore while he is driving is because he doesn't want to spill any.

94. Duke is one of the few ACC schools where football players are assigned their own personal bail bondsmen.

95. Duke announced the installation of a new voice-mail system at the campus suicide prevention center.

96. In the future, no Duke football player will be given a letter until he can read.

97. Joe Alleva has willed his ego to medical science.

98. Duke athletes believe in the two-party system: Party all day and party all night.

99. Coach K's doctor recently told him to eat more vegetables, so he started putting two olives in every martini.

100. Kathleen Smith never met a mirror she didn't like.

101. The only time Mike Cragg is ever speechless is when someone asks him the last time he skipped a meal.

102. A list of 10 most admired women by Duke sorority members: Monica Lewinsky.

103. Ricki Lake.

104. Monica Lewinsky.

105. Paula Jones.

106. Monica Lewinsky.

107. Linda Tripp.

108. Janet Reno.

109. Cathleen Willie.

110. Monica Lewinsky.

111. My sorority president.

112. Dr. Nannerl Koehane is next on a waiting list for a charisma bypass.

113. Carl Franks is so dense he once studied for a blood test.

114. Bob Trott is so mean he once showed his kid a picture taken at Mickey Mouse's funeral.

115. To graduate, Duke football players must complete a remedial reading program in "Trash Talk."

116. Duke players considered a revolt when athletic officials wouldn't allow beer to be served at breakfast.

117. Duke takes pride that nearly 67 percent of its former players have been granted parole before the end of their sentence.

118. The NCAA has moved a branch office to the Duke campus to cut down on travel expenses.

119. Duke coaches have drills during spring practice in "Finger-pointing at your opponent."

120. Winter conditioning drills at Duke also include a course in "The proper way to shoot the bird."

121. A survey of 75,000 Durham residents revealed that 90 percent believed Duke was a private school. This result was largely attributed to the fact that the football team plays like one.

122. The remaining 10 percent did not know Duke had a football team.

123. Christian Laettner is living proof that you don't need a three-digit I.Q. to graduate from Duke.

124. The reason athletic officials won't install real grass on the playing field is because they are concerned the cheerleaders will graze too often.

125. Barry Wilson's greatest contribution to the Duke football program was leaving.

126. The fact that Wallace Wade Stadium seats 33,000 proves how little there is to do in Durham.

127. The Duke campus would make a nice nuclear waste dump.

128. When Steve Spurrier left Duke for Florida, the I.Q. of both places doubled.

129. Duke men refuse to marry kin unless they are at least third cousins.

130. Coach K never met a chili dog he didn't like.

131. Duke law students have posters of their hero, Richard Nixon, in their dorm rooms.

132. Duke likes to brag it has one of the top law schools in America. Like somebody else would want one.

133. The best-selling book at the Duke campus bookstore this winter will be *I Hate North Carolina.*

134. The second best-selling book will be *I Hate Paul Finebaum.*

135. The best-selling bumper sticker in Durham reads, "Honk if you turned down the Duke coaching job."

136. The choice of car among Duke basketball players is the K car.

137. Jesse Helms will be the guest of honor at the next spring game.

138. The FDA is considering allowing recordings of the Carl Franks show to be used in place of sleeping pills.

139. The Duke coaching staff had to separate Wives' Day and Girlfriends' Day because a couple of guys brought both.

140. Three things DUKE stands for: Dumb Uneducated Klutzy Eggheads.

141. Devils Usually Keep Enemies.

142. Disaster Under K's Eyes.

143. The Duke campus doesn't need a comedy club. All students need to do for a laugh is look at the non-conference schedule in the ACC.

144. Caning must be legal in Chapel Hill because the Blue Devils get beaten every year they play there.

145. A number of Duke fans are convinced Dean Smith is related to Saddam Hussein.

146. There is something to be said for Coach K, and he is usually saying it.

147. Alumni believe a Rhodes Scholar is a student traveling down Campus Drive.

148. Duke basketball players believe a fast-break is leaving a 7-Eleven without paying.

149. The top five choices for commencement speaker: Beavis.

150. Butthead.

151. Eric Cartman.

152. Paul Finebaum.

153. Bart Simpson.

154. The hotels are so bad near the Duke campus that to get room service you have to dial 911.

155. The top five reasons students chose to attend Duke: Like ugly women.

156. UNC was full.

157. Wanted to go to a school that didn't play major college football.

158. Their parents didn't want them to be distracted by watching the football team on national television.

159. Enjoyed being around people with acne.

160. Fans believe Duke's quarterback is blind. What other explanation is there for always throwing the ball to the other team?

161. School administrators are relieved they didn't name the law school after Richard Nixon when he became president.

162. Carl Franks secretly wants to coach at Florida.

163. The best-selling placard every year at the end of the UNC game is "Wait until next year."

164. The captain of the Duke cheerleading squad is determined by the girl with the smallest fever blister.

165. The food in the Durham campus restaurants is so bad the only card they take is Blue Cross.

166. Coach K was once dropped as a member of the human race.

167. Duke fans won't visit Mount Rushmore because Coach K's face isn't featured.

168. The Duke homecoming queen was so ugly she had to wear a turtleneck to cover her flea collar.

169. Barry Wilson left Duke after several years complaining of illness and fatigue. The fans were sick and tired of him.

170. Coach K once said, "Our society doesn't need to get rid of our coaches. Instead, we need to find away to get rid of our alumni."

171. Instead of using a driver's license for admission, graduates may now show their Duke diploma for entrance into Wallace Wade Stadium.

172. Some Duke coeds are so fat they have unlisted dress sizes.

173. Some Duke cheerleaders are so ugly they are often mistaken for circus animals.

174. After losing again to UNC, Coach K said, "If lessons are learned in defeat, our team is getting a great education."

175. Duke graduates get a "get out of jail free" card when they graduate; they'll need it if they go to work for Congress.

176. Vic Bubas learned humility at Duke.

177. Duke has a graduate class titled "How to be a nerd."

178. The 10 most hated sportswriters in North Carolina: Dave Droschek.

179. Jimmy DuPree.

180. Al Featherston.

181. Steve Riley.

182. A.J. Carr.

183. Caulton Tudor.

184. Stuart Hall.

185. Harry Pickett.

186. Ron Green.

187. Greg Doyel.

188. Janet Reno was once captain of the Duke cheerleading squad.

189. The Blue Devils have a bowl tradition of staying home.

190. Like a broken-down horse, Coach K ought to be shot and put out of his misery.

191. Coach K is next in line for a brain transplant.

192. The worst profession in the state of North Carolina is dentistry.

193. The best thing you can say about Duke is that it's not in South Carolina.

194. Only 12 percent of Duke students have ever owned a bottle of shampoo.

195. The leaves begin to fall every autumn about the same time the Duke football program does.

196. Duke cheerleaders only have sex on days that end in "y."

197. The television show *America's Most Wanted* was based on the Duke basketball team.

198. The men at Duke have so little understanding of pretty women that posters of The Fabulous Sports Babe are often seen on dorm room walls.

199. The most feared words for any Duke cheerleader are "Sorry, honey, we just ran out of cheese puffs."

200. Last year's homecoming queen was so ugly that when they took her to the top of Wallace Wade Stadium she was attacked by a plane.

201. Duke fans are such rednecks they name their children after stock car racers.

202. The only thing that could make the Duke basketball team happier than winning the national championship is if they made marijuana legal.

203. Before declaring a major, freshmen at Duke are required to declare their favorite Beastie Boy.

204. Coach K is a dork.

205. The Duke liberal arts school has a foreign language requirement for in-state students: English.

206. Some Duke basketball players went ahead and enlisted last year instead of waiting for NBA draft day.

207. Carl Franks says, "The best thing about football is that it only takes four quarters to finish a fifth."

208. Carl Franks is known to nap during the fourth quarter of big games.

209. It is a misdemeanor for Duke players to snort the chalk lines on the practice field.

210. Carl Franks went swimming in Loch Ness and the monster got out.

211. The Duke halftime show has been featured on *America's Funniest Home Videos.*

212. The common belief by Duke alumni is that the ABC series *Coach* is based on the career of Carl Franks.

213. What do you call it when the Blue Devil football team has three players quit the team in one seven-day stretch? A good week.

214. Duke's colors are blue and white, but after playing UNC they are usually black and blue.

215. Duke students believe Bedrock Residents Hall was named after the Flintstones.

216. Duke brags about its large number of academic all-Americans. That just means their jocks understand exactly why they are losers.

217. Pick-up line heard at a local Duke bar: "For a fat girl, you really don't sweat much."

218. Duke girl's response: "Thanks."

219. If it wasn't for pickpockets, Duke fraternity members wouldn't have a sex life.

220. What do Duke girls make for dinner? Reservations.

221. Steve Spurrier said his fondest memory of the Duke campus was in his rearview mirror.

222. Coach K got the Duke job because he was the only candidate to spell his name right on the application.

223. They once tried to mate a Duke cheerleader with a pig. But there are some things even a pig won't do.

224. First place in a recent Duke radio giveaway was a pair of football season tickets.

225. Second place were two pairs of tickets.

226. The Duke quarterback is believed to be color-blind. What other explanation is there for always throwing the ball to the other team?

227. How can you have a first-rate school when it changes football coaches more often than some people change underwear?

228. Duke resembles a country club more than any other college in the nation.

229. It's too bad Duke graduates end up working in them.

230. Bob Trott took the worst defense in the ACC and made it the worst in the country.

231. Duke students know they're drunk when they get sick in the stands and it's still not as disgusting as what's happening on the field.

232. An earthquake ripped through Durham during a homecoming football game, totally destroying the seats in the student section at Wallace Wade Stadium. Fortunately, no one was injured.

233. Duke is the biggest joke in the NCAA.

234. Former coach Steve Spurrier was the biggest jerk to pass through Durham.

235. Or the state of North Carolina.

236. Or, for that matter, the entire universe.

237. O. J. Simpson could have gone to Durham after he escaped from the police because no one would have ever thought to look for a football player there.

238. A good season at Duke is not being investigated by the NCAA.

239. Christian Laettner had difficulty making enemies at Duke because his friends hated him so much.

240. Popular saying by Duke football players: "A tie is like kissing a North Carolina girl."

241. The only good thing about Duke is that since nobody knows where it is, few people get to see what a dump it is.

242. The captain of the Duke cheerleading squad recently had her home phone number posted on the men's room of the athletic dorm.

243. The Campus Drive hooker is a virgin.

244. If Joe Alleva had been captain of the *Titanic,* he would have told the passengers they were just stopping for ice.

245. Football games at Duke are so boring that pigeons fly into the broadcast booth and think the announcers are statues.

246. Carl Frank's favorite expression: "The past isn't what it used to be."

247. They can't start Happy Hour in Durham until sportswriter Jimmy DuPree leaves the room.

248. The favorite television show at the athletic dorm is *Gomer Pyle, USMC.*

249. Duke football players think Dr. Kevorkian is the team doctor.

250. Some Duke cornerbacks confuse the term "nickel-back" with "nickel-bag."

251. Some Duke cheerleaders are so ugly they have to get prescription bathing suits.

252. A Blue Devil with half a brain is considered gifted.

253. The only sure thing in life is that Duke won't win the ACC in football.

254. If two Duke students jump off a cliff, which one hits the ground first? The one carrying the stolen television.

255. Duke players can do practically everything with a basketball but sign it.

256. The Blue Devil is the dumbest mascot in the ACC.

257. The Bryan Student Center is a nice location for a new stadium.

258. The captain of the Duke cheerleading team was voted most likely to conceive.

259. Some Duke coeds don't shave under their arms.

260. The girls who don't shave under their arms are the most popular with the engineering students.

261. The home economics school offers a course called "How to avoid sex after marriage."

262. A press guide is someone who helps the media find Duke's campus.

263. Duke fans consider a license plate personalized if it's made by a former Blue Devil player in prison.

264. Fans think that two people have walked on water and one of them coached at Duke.

265. The student newspaper, *The Chronicle,* serves its purpose during Durham's toilet paper shortages.

266. Elizabeth Dole could have started on the Duke football team.

267. Coach K has instituted a "Don't ask, don't tell" policy among recruits.

268. The only difference between Joe Alleva and a brick wall is the wall has some personality.

269. Say this about Coach K: He is as graceless in defeat as he is in victory.

270. The following are a list of Cherokee Parks' favorite pastimes at Duke: Drinking.

271. Chasing women.

272. Skipping class.

273. Drinking more.

274. Chasing more women.

275. Skipping most classes.

276. Drinking all day.

277. Chasing every woman.

278. Skipping every class.

279. All of the above.

280. Coach K's biggest fear in life is male-pattern baldness.

281. The only time Coach K doesn't look in a mirror is when he's pulling out of a parking place.

282. The only thing growing faster than the national debt is Coach K's waistline.

283. The Durham police often borrow Duke players for lineups to make the setting more realistic.

284. Duke has never won a national championship in football but has ranked high during that time in NCAA investigations.

285. Joe Alleva is the kind of person who goes to an orgy and complains about the cheese dip.

286. Happiness is seeing Durham in your rearview mirror.

287. Bug-zappers with Dean Smith's picture on them are hot sellers this year in Durham.

288. Three job possibilities for Carl Franks after leaving the Duke football program: Work for Goldsmith jewelers.

289. Talk to his college pal Steve Spurrier to see if they could switch jobs.

290. Make photocopies of his *Sports Illustrated* covers and fax them to other schools.

291. Since they are so popular, Duke officials ought to consider putting steroid dispensers in the football locker room.

292. Duke has a graduate course on "How to avoid marrying your next of kin."

293. The school also has a course in "What to do if you have."

294. Coach K can say absolutely nothing and mean it.

295. Joe Alleva always has two seats in the athletic director's box: One for himself and one for his ego.

296. Grant Hill once said, "If we didn't have to go to class, this really would have been a cool school."

297. Coach K is so dull he lights up a room when he leaves it.

298. Blue Devils are proof of reincarnation, because you can't get that dumb in just one lifetime.

299. Blue Devils have to climb chain link fences to see what's on the other side.

300. Coach K has a pin-up of Marcia Clark in his office.

301. Some Duke students believe the book *How the Grinch Stole Christmas* is about the Duke-UNC series.

302. If Coach K ever writes a book, it might be titled: *I Hate Paul Finebaum and Here Are 303 reasons Why You Should, Too.*

303. The Blue Devil calls all the plays from the sidelines.